Puffin Books
Houdini's Book of Ma

Even now 'Houdini' is a h........u name –
indication of just how great a magician he was.
Fifty years after his death, his achievements still
inspire people to become magicians and
illusionists themselves; this is just the book to help
you on your way . . .

Ben Hamilton presents a variety of Houdini's
tricks, from the very simple things he did as an
apprentice magician to the mind-boggling illusions
he created in later years. All the tricks are
carefully graded and each one has the 'patter' he
used in presenting them on stage.

With all this, a child of nine to eleven can have
hours of fun and learn to be as magical as
Houdini himself.

Houdini's
Book of Magic

The secrets of Harry Houdini,
the world's greatest man of magic

Compiled by Ben Hamilton
Illustrated by Raymond Turvey

Puffin Books

Puffin Books, Penguin Books Ltd, Harmondsworth,
Middlesex, England
Penguin Books, 625 Madison Avenue,
New York, New York 10022, U.S.A.
Penguin Books Australia Ltd, Ringwood,
Victoria, Australia
Penguin Books Canada Ltd, 2801 John Street,
Markham, Ontario, Canada L3R 1B4
Penguin Books (N.Z.) Ltd, 182–190 Wairau Road,
Auckland 10, New Zealand

First published 1982
Reprinted 1982

Made and printed in Great Britain by
Richard Clay (The Chaucer Press) Ltd, Bungay, Suffolk
Set in Linotype Baskerville

Contents

Four Star Magic 53

Five Star Magic 69

The Great Houdini 83

Introduction

Harry Houdini was probably the best-known man of magic in the history of the world. Even now, more than fifty years after his death, his name is still a household word.

Born as Erich Weiss, he was an American conjuror who became an international celebrity as a dare-devil escapologist and master illusionist. He was a great showman and a superb magician and this book contains the very best of his secrets.

Houdini was known as the 'Man of Many Secrets', the first of which seems to have been the date and place of his birth! He was probably born in Budapest in Hungary on 24 March 1874. In later years, he celebrated his birthday on 6 April and claimed Appleton, Wisconsin, as his birthplace. Certainly, it was either immediately before or immediately after his birth that his parents left Hungary and emigrated to the United States. His father, Mayer Samuel Weiss, was a rabbi, with a wife called Cecilia who was twenty years his junior. They had six children, five sons and a daughter – and they were poor but not starving.

The details of Houdini's boyhood aren't easy to establish, but a few facts are known: in 1888 the Weiss family moved from Wisconsin to New York, where they lived in a small flat at 305 East 69th Street; in 1892 Rabbi Weiss died and the family had to fend for itself. For a while in his teens Harry had been apprenticed to a locksmith, but by the the time of his father's death he had already launched himself as a 'man of magic'.

Legend has it that Harry was first bitten by the magic bug when his father took him to see an English magician called Doctor Lyn who toured the States in the 1880s. Doctor Lyn's most spectacular effect involved 'chloroforming' a patient and then cutting off his arms, legs and head – only to restore them at the end of the trick! The story goes that this inspired young Harry to attempt some spectacular effects of his own – in the first of which he would hang upside-down and pick up needles with his eyelashes! When he was still a small boy this remarkable acrobatic feat is said to have secured him a brief engagement with Jack Hoeffner's Five Cent Circus when it passed through Appleton.

With great enthusiasm the young Houdini was also doing his best to master some rather more basic magic. When he was seventeen, he turned 'professional': he and his brother Theo set themselves up as an act called 'The Houdini Brothers'. They borrowed the name from the famous nineteenth-century French magician and illusionist Robert-Houdin. The first job the brothers got was at Huber's Dime Museum on 14th Street in New York. They had to give twenty performances a day for very little reward, but it was a start. Card tricks were the basis of their act, but fellow performers taught them some elementary 'rope tie artistry' and 'handcuff manipulation' and before long they had scraped together enough money to buy a trick 'substitution trunk' that had been invented by the English magician Maskelyne in 1865. Having given it an exotic name – 'Metamorphosis' – the brothers took it on tour.

It is used in a trick which is still performed today and is still very striking: the person standing on the lid of the locked trunk instantly changes place with the person *inside* the trunk; what's more, the person inside the trunk has been handcuffed, tied up in a sack and then locked in the trunk by one of the audience! The secret is an ingeniously constructed trapdoor in the lid; though not visible to the audience, it allows the instant change to happen.

When the Houdini Brothers were appearing in Coney Island they met Beatrice Rahner, a young singer and dancer. Bess and Harry fell in love and were married on 22 June 1894. A few weeks after the wedding Theo went his own way as 'Professor Houdini', an act that was not a success, and Bess joined Harry as 'The Houdinis'.

In their early years together, the Houdinis may not have been very successful or lucky, but Harry was certainly determined and they managed to get work of sorts in circuses and at fairground side-shows.

When they were on tour with the Welsh Brothers' Circus in Chicago in 1898, Harry had an idea. One of the most popular features of his act was the way he managed to escape from ropes and handcuffs attached to him by members of the audience. As he had been apprenticed to a locksmith, and as he spent all day practising handcuff escapes, maybe he could be handcuffed and locked in the local prison cell and yet escape?

The local police agreed to go along with the idea, although to make sure there were no duplicate keys smuggled into the cell they had Harry stripped of all his clothes. For years Harry had been training his fingers to enable him to escape from handcuffs, so escaping from the regulation police handcuffs was easy enough, but what about the doors to the cell? As everyone left the cell, a parting good-luck kiss from Bess ensured that a small skeleton key was passed from her mouth to his!

When Harry Houdini managed to escape from that Chicago police cell, the police were amazed – and the newspapers turned it into a big story. The publicity helped the Houdinis enormously. They got more work and better work.

In 1900 Harry made his first trip to Europe. By now he had learned how important publicity was, so he knew that the first place for him to visit in London was a police cell at Scotland Yard. He had discovered that the regulation handcuffs of the British police would release themselves if tapped sharply on a hard surface, so escape from them would be simple. Once again, Bess gave him a good-luck kiss as she left the cell. Once again he escaped. Once again the Press were amazed and very impressed. Indeed, such was the publicity that Harry's one-week booking at the Alhambra Theatre in London was extended to several months. In 1900 and 1901 he toured most of the United Kingdom and much of Europe; for the rest of his life he remained a firm favourite with British audiences. In 1911 he became first president of the Magicians' Club of London, the forerunner of the Magic Circle; he retained this august office until his death.

Houdini's great successes in Europe were followed by even greater successes in America. He was now a star – but to stay a star he had to work very hard indeed. Every day he worked with weights and took ice-cold baths. Bess had to pour more and more ice blocks into his bath to ensure absolute safety for his escapes from crates flung into cold harbours and rivers. Sometimes the ice had to be broken before the escapes could proceed. Some of his rivals stole his escape ideas, thinking them easy, not bothering with the heavy training schedule. They drowned themselves. Hard training was essential. What's more, he never left anything to chance. The Great Houdini's motto was 'Safety first'.

Inevitably, his public demanded that each thrill be capped by a greater thrill the next year! In 1908 he escaped from a packing case flung into the Mississippi by the New Orleans police. Later in the same year he escaped from a massive safe at London's Euston Palace of Varieties –

complete with reinforced stage, so massively heavy was
the safe. His escape took three minutes. In various theatres,
he 'walked through a brick wall', he escaped from a solid-
stone tower, from a padlocked leather mail-bag, from a
milk can full of water, and, knowing he must improve on
even that, he was locked upside-down in a tankful of
water only to appear – drenched but triumphant – four
minutes later.

The spectacular illusions that had been added to the
act, which was now called 'Houdini's Magical Revue',
needed considerable scenery and props. Sometimes as many
as ten railway wagons were required to transport them
from town to town. He and Bess played the top theatres
and stayed in the top hotels, though even in this luxury he
made sure he trained hard every day. He was now accepted
as the greatest illusionist and escape artist of all time.

In 1919 he went to Hollywood and made several silent
films. In *The Master Mystery* he was the secret agent hero
Quentin Locke. In fifteen-minute episodes he was threatened
by the 'Automaton', a robot that infected its victims with a
disease called 'Madagascar Madness'! Other series such as
The Grim Game and *Terror Island* followed.

By now he was in his forties; as he grew older, his
feats grew more spectacular, not less so. He gave no sign of
tiring. In 1926, when he was fifty-two, in a challenge to the
fakir Rhaman Bey, he stayed under water for seventy-five
minutes – fifteen minutes longer than the fakir – incarcerated
in the lead container that was destined to become his coffin.

On 18 October 1926 he was playing the Palace Theatre,
Montreal, when an over-enthusiastic student from the local
university accepted his light-hearted challenge to hit him
hard in the stomach. The Great Houdini was as fit as ever.
The student hit him, but before Houdini had time to
tense his muscles in readiness for the blow. He was in
pain, but the show must go on. At the next theatre on the

tour, the Garrick at Detroit, despite the increasing pain, he insisted on being lowered into the water for his Chinese Water Torture Cell trick. No sooner was he inside the tank than he gave the danger signal. He was dragged from the tank and rushed to hospital. The ruptured appendix was removed, but peritonitis set in. He died on 31 October 1926. He was buried in a grave in New York's Macpehah Cemetery – the final resting place of the Great Houdini – over which was placed the elaborate monument he had designed himself.

Houdini may have died more than half a century ago, but his magic lives on – and is as exciting as ever. The first forty tricks you will find in this book are all ones that with patience and practice you should be able to master and perform. Naturally, the One Star Magic in the book is a lot simpler to understand and easier to do than the Five Star Magic, but all the tricks are ones that an amateur magician should be able to do just as well as Houdini himself once did. The stunts and illusions in the last chapter, however, are ones that you *won't* be able to do! They include some of the remarkable feats that made Houdini famous – from escaping from a locked safe to sawing a lady in half – and they are included so that you can discover how the Great Houdini did them, not so you can try to do them yourself.

Each piece of magic is presented in Houdini's own words; when you are presenting the tricks for your family and friends you can use his 'patter' – which is what magicians call the words they speak when performing a trick. With each trick there is a list of the 'props' you will need. These are the bits and pieces that you will be using in the trick; most of them are very simple things you will find around the house. At the start of the description of each trick there is also information about the number of 'assistants' and 'helpers' required. The 'assistants' are friends who are 'in the know'. The 'helpers' are volunteers from the audience who you hope won't discover your secrets. Audiences can be as large as you like.

If you want to put on the Greatest Magic Show on Earth, everything you need to know can be found in this book – thanks to the world's greatest man of magic, the one and only Harry Houdini.

One Star Magic ✳

These tricks are easy ones: it won't take you long to master them and you only need a few very simple props and a little bit of practice.

Have fun!

The Magic Coins

Props: Two coins
Assistants: None
Helpers: One

The Trick

For my first piece of magic I need a helper from the audience. Do I have any volunteers?

Good – please step this way. Now, I want you to take these two coins, one in each hand, and in a moment – when I've gone out of the room – hold one coin up in front of your eyes and the other on your knee, and count to twenty.

When I come back into the room, I'll tell you which hand held the coin up to your face and which hand held the coin on your knee.

It sounds impossible, but I can do it!

The Secret

When I returned, I could see that one hand was a bit redder, the other a bit whiter, than usual. Blood had drained into the hand held on the knee, but out of the hand held up to your eyes. Even when you relaxed your hands, the colour difference was still there.

The Magic Telephone

Props: Six cards and a telephone
Assistants: One
Helpers: One

The Trick

Ladies and gentlemen, here are six cards, which I am going to lay face up on the table. As you can see, they are:

The Ace of Spades
The Ten of Hearts
The Jack of Diamonds
The Queen of Clubs
The Four of Spades
The Seven of Hearts

Now I'd like a volunteer from the audience to come and choose just one of the six cards. You've chosen the Ten of Hearts. Good. Now please go over to the telephone and dial 12345.

When the phone is answered, ask for Mr Lacey and ask him what card you have chosen. Believe it or not, he'll give you the right answer.

The Secret

The person who answers the telephone is an accomplice, of course. (The number given in the trick is merely an example.) When you ring up and ask for Mr Lacey, all he has to do is look at a list he has in front of him and tell you the card you've chosen.

Mr Jones means the Ace of Spades
Mr Lacey means the Ten of Hearts
Mr Roberts means the Jack of Diamonds
Mr Archer means the Queen of Clubs
Mr Simon means the Four of Spades
Mr Smith means the Seven of Hearts

When you choose the Ten of Hearts, he's Mr Lacey. When you choose the Ace of Spades, he's Mr Jones. When you choose the Jack of Diamonds, he's Mr Roberts. And so on.

You need a good memory to perform this trick because you've got to be able to remember which name belongs to which card. And it is a trick you should perform only once in a while at very special magic shows because every telephone call you make costs money.

The Magic Postcard

Props: A postcard and eight coins
Assistants: None
Helpers: One

The Trick

For this trick I need one volunteer from the audience to
come and hold out his or her hand for me.

Now, here is my magic postcard. I'll hold it in one
hand and place four coins on it. And if you will now hold
up your hand, I'll slide the four coins into your palm. That's
odd – *eight* coins are now in your hand!

The Secret

When I hold the postcard, I am already holding four
coins under it, pressed against the card with my finger.

When I slide the top four coins off into your hand, I also
release the hidden four – and that makes eight!

The Magic Hat

Props: A top hat, a glass tumbler and some coins
Assistants: None
Helpers: None

The Trick

All the best magicians have a top hat – and the Great
Houdini is no exception. I've got a top hat and a glass
tumbler and a handful of coins – and I'm going to make
one of the coins fall through the hat into the tumbler!

I carefully put the hat upside-down on the empty tumbler.
Then I drop the coins into the hat – and look, one of them
has gone right through the hat into the glass below!

The Secret

When I carefully put the hat upside-down on the empty glass, I took a bit of time doing it. As I balanced the hat on the glass, so, with my other hand – as though straightening the hat – I was slipping a coin between the rim of the glass and the hat. Now I make sure I *do* drop the coins into the hat, because the vibration dislodges the hidden coin and it falls into the glass tumbler – and the audience bursts into thunderous applause!

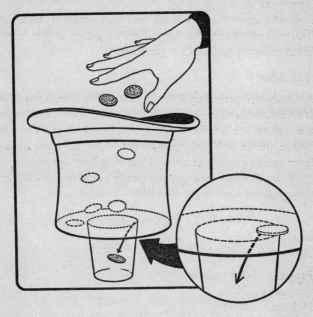

The Magic Orange

Props: A bowl of oranges, a knife and a penny
Assistants: None
Helpers: One

The Trick

Here's a bowl of juicy oranges; I want a volunteer from the audience to come and choose one and hand it to me. This one? Right.

I take your magic orange and this ordinary knife and I cut the orange in two. Hey, there's a penny in the orange, look! How on earth did it get there?

The Secret

If I hold the penny against the blade of the knife you'll see it's not as wide as the blade. In other words, you couldn't see the penny behind the blade when I picked the knife up. Before the trick I had already got a dab of soap, pressed it on to the blade and pressed the coin into the soap.

When I cut the orange, the penny came off and fell into the open orange!

The Magic Apple

Props: Two apples
Assistants: None
Helpers: One

The Trick

This is a piece of magic that's going to prove to you that the Great Houdini has superhuman strength. As you can see, I have two apples. Here is one of them. See if you can break it in two with your bare hands. Try a bit harder. You can't manage it? The truth is that it needs an incredible amount of strength given only to the Great Houdini. Watch me do it – there!

The Secret

It needs no strength at all! It needs the treatment I gave to *my* apple and didn't give to *your* apple. I took a needle

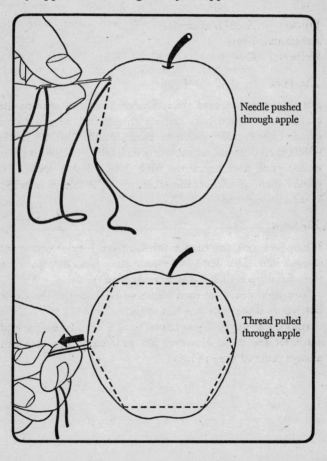

Needle pushed
through apple

Thread pulled
through apple

threaded with strong thread and I pushed it in and out of the skin round the apple. Then I pulled on the ends of the thread and this cut the apple beneath the skin, so that breaking it was easy.

The Magic Card

Props: A pack of cards
Assistants: None
Helpers: One

The Trick

For this, my first card trick, I need a volunteer from the audience to come and inspect this brand new pack of cards. Now kindly choose a card. Right. Don't tell me which card it is, but let me study its back . . . Now return it to the pack and watch me find the card you chose. I'll spread them all out on the table, so . . . is this your card? It is? I thought so!

The Secret

When you took the card from the pack I expressed great interest in it. This was to take your attention away from the rest of the pack that I was secretly *bending*!

You then put your card back; when I spread the cards out, yours is the only one not slightly curved.

And don't worry if you haven't got a brand new pack of cards for the trick. However old your cards are, you can always pretend they're new!

The Magic Golf Ball

Props: Two golf balls
Assistants: None
Helpers: None

The Trick

I've got two golf balls here and I'm going to do something really remarkable with them ... Watch ...

Even expert jugglers find the feat of balancing one golf ball on top of another almost impossible ... but I think I can manage it ... I've been practising a lot ... there you are, I've done it – one ball on top of the other!

The Secret

It's so easy when you know how.

I put a dab of soap on one of the golf balls and press the other against it; it will 'balance' for as long as I want!

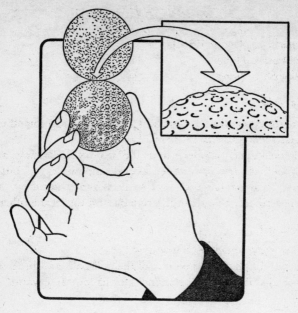

Two Star Magic **

These tricks aren't quite so easy. To master
them calls for patience and practice. Read the
instructions carefully before trying them out
and rehearse them over and over again before
you show them to an audience.

For several of the tricks you will need special
props, but they are all quite simple and can be
made out of everyday things you will find around
the house. Good luck!

This is Your Card!

Props: A pack of cards
Assistants: None
Helpers: One

The Trick

I'm holding out a few playing cards and would like a volunteer from the audience to select one card, look at it and give it back to me without letting me see what it is. Thanks – now I take it and place it with the others. Now, watch me find your card . . . This is your card – the Eight of Spades!

The Secret

The secret lies in the cards I allowed you to choose from. I took from the pack the three, five, six, seven, eight and nine of spades, clubs and hearts – *not* diamonds. How do these particular cards help a magician?

On each of these cards, the majority of pips (that's what we call the little heart, club and spade shapes on the cards) point one way. Before starting the trick, I make sure that all the cards have the majority of pips pointing in the same direction; when I put the chosen card back with the others, I turn it round.

Then when I spread all the cards out on the table, I can see at once which card has the majority of pips pointing the wrong way.

The Mystery Card

Props: A pack of cards and a plain, thin handkerchief
Assistants: None
Helpers: One

The Trick

Take a card and show it to your neighbour, so there's no doubt as to which card you've taken. And now may I take it back from you? Thanks. I will return it to the pack.

I'm going to put the cards safely under cover by placing them on the table and covering them with a handkerchief.

Right, I've done that . . . and the card you chose was the Two of Clubs! I knew I was right!

The Secret

I asked you to show the card to your neighbour so that you wouldn't notice me *turning over* the bottom card of the pack. Now I hold the pack out to you with that bottom card uppermost and you assume that every card is facing downwards as usual.

When you returned the card, all I had to do was turn over the pack once more and spread out the cards on a table while I covered them with a big handkerchief. The card I reversed and the card you returned to the pack are the only ones facing upwards, so I can easily see your card through the handkerchief!

The Disappearing Handkerchiefs

Props: A home-made paper bag and four
            handkerchiefs
Assistants: None
Helpers: None

The Trick

Here is an ordinary paper bag and here are two handkerchiefs. As you can see, the paper bag has nothing in it –
please look inside it carefully. In fact, I will turn the bag
inside out! I have nothing to hide – both the bag and the
two handkerchiefs are straightforward.

I put the handkerchiefs in my trouser pocket, say the
magic word *Abracadabra!* – and the handkerchiefs have
gone! To prove this, let me pull out my pocket lining and
show you that the pocket is empty.

So where are the handkerchiefs? Incredibly, they are now
in the empty paper bag and I will take them out . . . if I
can . . . yes, here they are!

The Secret

First, I put the handkerchiefs into my trouser pocket – or
rather into my trouser leg. For at the top of the pocket
(where it will not be noticed) is a cut in the lining and my
handkerchiefs were pushed through that cut. I then seemed
to have had a struggle taking the handkerchiefs from
the bag. That struggle is deliberate, as there is one bag
inside another and the tops of the two bags are glued
together. I had to tear the inside paper bag and take out
the handkerchiefs that had been hidden between the two
layers of paper bag!

The Magic Loops

Props: Red, white and blue loops of paper about
              50 cm long, a piece of string and a special
              handkerchief
Assistants: None
Helpers: Two

The Trick

Here I have a piece of string; hanging from it are three
loops of paper – one red, one white and one blue.

If you and your friend will each hold one end of the string,
I'll throw this large handkerchief over the three paper loops
and the string.

Okay, tell me which loop you'd like me to choose. The
red one? Right, I'll find it under the handkerchief, pull it
free of the string, show it to you – except that, look, it is still
a whole loop! I never had to tear the loop to get it off the
string! How did I do it? It's pure magic, of course!

The Secret

It is anything but pure magic, of course!

The secret is underneath the handkerchief, in pockets
sewn on to the handkerchief, though inside it. When one of
you asked me for the red loop, I took the red loop off the
line by reaching underneath the handkerchief, tearing the
red loop (so taking it off the string) and, after removing the
duplicate from the pocket in the handkerchief, I put the
other (torn) loop into the pocket. I then held up the untorn
red loop – and you thought it was all pure magic. At least, I
hope you did.

The Mind Reader

Props: Some envelopes, some paper, a pencil and
            some carbon paper
Assistants: None
Helpers: None

The Trick

I'll hand you a bunch of envelopes, with an elastic band
round them to prove they are fresh from the stationer's. And
please take this pencil and bit of paper as well.

Now on the bit of paper I want you to write a secret
message. Right. Now I'll take back the envelopes; fold
your message *several times*.

Just a moment – I don't know what I'm thinking about
– I should have left one envelope with you so that you can
put the message in it! Anyway, here it is now.

Put your message in the envelope, seal it and put the
envelope in your pocket. Now I'm going to leave the room
for a moment to gather my thoughts – and to gather yours
at the same time!

I'm back ... and I can tell you your message was 'I
hate school dinners!'

Is that the message in the sealed envelope in your pocket?
I thought so!

The Secret

You wrote the message on a piece of paper that was on top
of a pile of envelopes. The top envelope had a piece of carbon
paper inside it. (Remember to put the carbon paper in the
envelope the right way round!) I then took back the
envelopes, only to remember that I should have let you
keep the top one so you could put your piece of paper in it.

But the envelope I gave back to you was not the top one,
because while you were busy folding your message several

times, I had put the top envelope at the bottom of the pile. When I went away to gather my thoughts, I opened the bottom envelope and read the carbon copy of your message.

The Vanishing Water

Props: A drinking glass, water, sticky tape and a
             straw
Assistants: None
Helpers: Two

The Trick

This is an ordinary drinking glass which I have half filled with water. I now put several strips of sticky tape across the top to make sure no one can drink the water.

Kindly switch off the lights and let me sit between you in the dark. When I say 'Now!', I want you on my right to hold the glass with one hand and *my* hand with the other. And you on my left do the same.

You will be holding the glass and both my hands, so there will be no way that I can remove the water from the glass. When I give the command, I want you both to count out loud up to 10. Here's the command! NOW!

1, 2, 3, 4, 5, 6, 7, 8, 9, 10. Now if someone will switch on the lights, they will see that all the water has vanished. But how?

The Secret

Just before giving the command, I had still got my hands free, so had taken a drinking straw from my inside pocket and put it in the glass through one of the gaps in the sticky tape under cover of darkness.

I then said 'Now!' and, though both my hands were held, it was easy for me to lean forward and drink from the straw.

The volunteers were counting so loudly that they couldn't hear me drinking. When I'd finished, I took up the straw with my mouth and let it drop to the floor, where it remained unnoticed when the lights were switched on again.

The Chinese Rope Trick

Props: Two lengths of string, each about 1 metre long
Assistants: None
Helpers: Two

The Trick

Can I have two volunteers from the audience who don't mind being tied together? They had better be friends, because the way I plan to tie them together, they may never part company again!

Here they come: two brave volunteers ready to rise to a challenge from the Great Houdini!

First, on my left, I'll tie your hands together with this long piece of string, leaving plenty of slack between your hands. Now, on my right, I'll tie *your* hands together in the same way. But, first, I must pass the loop of your string over the loop of hers, so that you are, in fact, tied together.

Now try to get apart, without cutting the string or untying the knots. You will find that you can't!

The Secret

In fact, you can! If I take the centre of the string holding your wrists, pass it through the loop of string on her left wrist and bring it down over her left hand, you will find yourselves separated! You don't believe me? Try it.

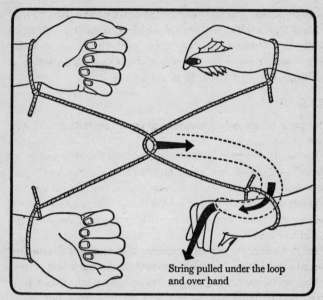

String pulled under the loop
and over hand

The Ancient Chinese used to tie their prisoners together like this – until an ancestor of mine came along and showed them that you can't tie down a Houdini!

Mark Your Card

Props: A pack of cards and a pencil
Assistants: None
Helpers: One

The Trick

Here's a new pack of cards. Please open the wrapper, inspect the cards carefully and shuffle them. Don't let me see what the card is, but choose one and hold on to it. In fact, mark it with a pencil! I'll take the pack now. See, I cut it. Now will you put your card back into the pack? Fine.

Now I've got to find out which is your card . . . I'll fan them out and have a look at their backs. It's a bit difficult for me – wait a second – I've got it! Is this your card that I'm holding up? I thought it might be!

The Secret

The pack of cards is genuinely new and so is the card you have chosen.

But while you pencil-marked your card I added one more special card to the pack. In fact, when you put your card back into the pack, you put it on top of my special card.

What's so special about it? Nothing that anyone except me would notice: a tiny crescent-shaped piece has been cut out of one end.

As I flipped through the cards, the moment I saw my special card I knew the one before it in the pack was yours!

You will only want to use a brand-new pack of cards on very special occasions. When you do this trick normally, you can use an ordinary pack of cards, but be sure to make your volunteer inspect the cards carefully so that he or she is completely convinced that the pack is unmarked before he or she chooses a card.

Three Star Magic ✳✳✳

These tricks are not difficult to perform, but most
of them require special props. They are props that
you can probably buy from a magic shop, but it is
much more fun to make your own – and, as a rule,
the magician who makes his own props tends to
understand how they work that much better and
consequently performs his tricks that much more
effectively. One or two of the props needed for the
tricks in this chapter will take some finding, but
they are worth trying to get hold of because they
will give your magic show that extra
professional polish. Good hunting!

The Magic Wand

Props: A special wand, an ordinary wand and
            some wrapping paper
Assistants: None
Helpers: None

The Trick

Ladies and gentlemen, look at my magic wand. It looks
like any other ordinary magician's wand, doesn't it? But it
isn't an ordinary wand. Far from it. This wand belongs to
the Great Houdini and is very, *very* special.

It's a handsome wand and a solid one. Let me bang it
on the table so you can hear how solid it is.

Now I am going to wrap it up in this pretty wrapping
paper . . . I've wrapped it up, but I promise it's still in
there – and as solid as ever, as you can hear when I bang it
on the table once more. But look, suddenly I crush the
wrapping paper and the wand into a very small ball.

So where has my magic wand gone? You think it's in this
crushed-up paper, but it can't be – the wand was solid.

Aha, here it is, in my inside pocket!

The Secret

The wand looks great with white ends and the centre part
of it black. When I tap it to show you how solid it is, I tap
one of the white ends, which are made of solid wood. The
black part is just tough black paper, so I can easily screw it
up into a small ball.

At the end of the trick I take a second wand, an ordinary
one, from my inside pocket, where it's been waiting all the
time.

The Wizard Wand

Props: A special wand
Assistants: None
Helpers: None

The Trick

Here's another wand, solid all through this time. This one
won't let us down and collapse into a paper ball. See, I
knock it on the table edge at the middle as well as the end
and hand it over safely to you.

Hey, what have you done? This one's collapsed just like
the last one!

The Secret

This one is indeed wooden all the way through, but it
isn't solid wood. It's hollow and made up of wooden sections
which are threaded together by a thick cord and, as you
can see now that I am holding it again, I have to push the
separate wooden blocks tight together along the cord and
hold them tight. If I don't, the wand collapses.

Cutting the Card

Props: A playing card, a pair of scissors and a
              business envelope with a flap on the short
              edge
Assistants: None
Helpers: None

The Trick

I put this playing card into this envelope. I seal the envelope
and *cut it in half* with this pair of scissors.

I now take the portions apart and hand you the card

– which is still uncut! But I have just cut the envelope with the card inside! I *must* have cut the card – but I didn't!

The Secret

Beforehand, I had made a slit on the under side of the envelope, the slit being parallel to the flap, halfway down the envelope and just a little bit wider than the playing card.

When I put the card in the envelope you didn't see the slit because it was underneath. So you saw me slide the card into the envelope, but you didn't see it slide partly *out* of the envelope again as it went through the slit.

Half the card was *out* of the envelope; when I cut the envelope in half, I cut *between* the card and the envelope so the card itself was never cut!

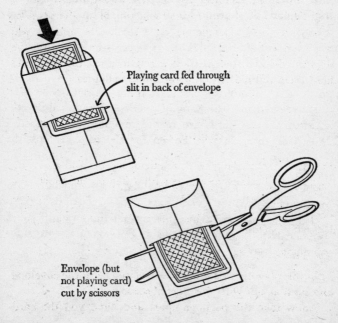

Playing card fed through slit in back of envelope

Envelope (but not playing card) cut by scissors

The King of Spades

Props: A special pack of cards
Assistants: None
Helpers: One

The Trick

Here is an ordinary pack of playing cards that you can
shuffle and cut as much as you like. However much shuffling
you do, when you hand the cards back to me, I'll find the
King of Spades for you, *instantly!*

Please, take the pack and shuffle it. I now take it back
from you; this card, when turned over, will, I hope, be the
King of Spades! It is!

Will you shuffle again? Now return the cards to me –
many thanks; I am sure *this* one must be the King. I'm
right again! But how do I find the King of Spades each and
every time?

The Secret

The secret is that my 'ordinary' pack of cards isn't ordinary
at all. Fifty-one of the cards are quite normal, to be sure,
but one of them – the King of Spades – is rather different.

Most playing cards are made from *two* pieces of card
glued together. In preparation for the trick, I took the
King of Spades and split it in two. Then I put a thin thread
inside the cardboard sandwich and glued the two pieces
of card together again. Once re-glued, I left a heavy weight
on the trick card for several days.

I now have a card that is just a small amount stiffer and
heavier than the others. *I* notice it, but no one else does, for
no one else is expecting it.

The Cards in the Hat

Props: Playing cards, envelopes, a top hat and a
            torch
Assistants: None
Helpers: Four

The Trick

Ladies and gentlemen, I want all the lights on for this
trick – I've got nothing to hide!

Now, sir, let me give you and your three friends a pack of
cards. Shuffle them and take a card each.

Now put each of your cards into separate envelopes and
seal them. You're most welcome to examine the cards and
the envelopes, because when I've finished this trick you're
bound to say it's something to do with the cards!

Okay, I'll collect up your four envelopes and bring them
over here to this top hat. Great. Now, I'm going to take one
of the envelopes out of this hat, press it against my forehead,
close my eyes and think hard for a second and . . . this card
is the Seven of Spades! Am I right? Yes, I thought I was!
I'll take the next envelope out of the hat and press it to my
forehead and think deeply . . . er . . . Ace of Hearts? Yes?
Good!

And now for the other two envelopes . . . the Three of
Clubs . . . the Nine of Hearts – I've done it!

The Secret

The secret has got nothing to do with mind reading, let
alone the magic of my pressing the envelopes to my forehead!

I've simply got a pile of *very thin* envelopes; you can also
buy thin playing cards, which is what I have done in this
case.

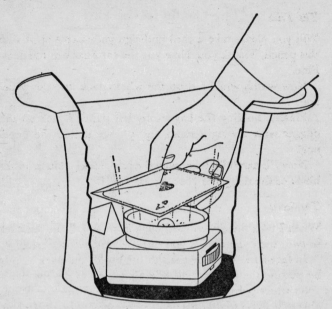

And why did I ask for the lights to be full on? It's so that you won't notice another light – a torch in the hat, to be precise. As I talk, I hold the envelope against the torch light inside the hat and I can see that the card is the Seven of Spades.

All that mumbo-jumbo about pressing the envelope to my forehead was just to fool you – and it did!

The Dagger and the Card

Props: A pack of cards, a 'dagger', a pencil and a
            paper bag
Assistants: None
Helpers: One

The Trick

Will you please take a card and sign your name on it with this pencil. Thank you. Now put the card back in the pack. Fine.

Now watch while I drop the whole pack into this paper bag.

Finally, holding the bag in my left hand, I pick up this dagger with my right hand and plunge it into the paper bag.

Now I'll carefully tear away the bag; look! – stuck on the blade of the dagger is your signed card!

The Secret

When I took the signed card back from you, I cut the pack in two; then you *thought* you put the card *into* the pack.

In fact I moved your card to the top of the pack simply by putting the bottom half of the pack on to the top half.

So when I dropped the entire pack into the bag, I was able to hold on to that particular card while also holding on to the folds of the paper bag; I then pressed it against the side of the bag.

Once I had stuck the dagger into the card, I used the dagger to pull the card away from the rest of the pack, deliberately tore the bag – and there was your card!

When you do the trick, don't use a real dagger or you'll end up getting hurt. A paper knife will do instead, or even a very sharp pencil. And if you don't want to spoil real playing cards, make some of your own out of stiff paper. In fact, paper 'cards' work well with this trick because they are easier to pierce.

The Vanishing Balls

Props: A special handkerchief, a small rubber ball
             and a hat
Assistants: None
Helpers: None

The Trick

I am holding up a handkerchief for you to look at. As you
can see, it's empty. I crumple it up, so – and from it I take
out this rubber ball! Then I drop the ball into the hat
underneath the handkerchief.

Although the handkerchief is now empty – and I'm
holding it up to show you it is – when I crumple it up again,
another ball appears! I'll drop that second ball into the hat
as well.

Let me do this once more – there, we have three balls in
the hat; I will now hand you the hat to examine. What do
you mean, there are *no balls* in the hat? There should be
three! There *were* three – but they've vanished!

The Secret

Each time I hold up the handkerchief, I hold the two top
corners and I don't show you the other side of the handkerchief. If I did, you would see that hanging in the middle is
one rubber ball, attached to the hem by a colourless thread.

There is one ball only, used three times! The three balls
you thought you saw were the same one. After I drop the
ball into the hat each time, I lift it out again when I
straighten out the handkerchief. When I crumple up the
handkerchief, I pick the ball out of the middle of it without
letting you see the thread.

Practise this trick until you've mastered it and you'll
really mystify your friends.

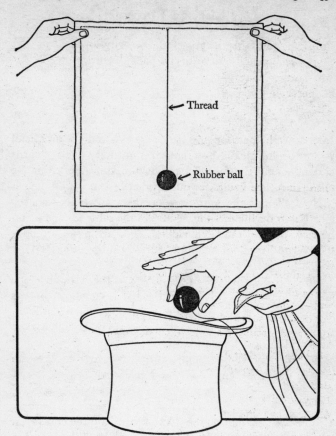

← Thread

← Rubber ball

Change Places

Props: A table, a tablecloth, two envelopes, a
            pencil and a special pack of cards
Assistants: None
Helpers: Two

The Trick

I need two helpers for this piece of magic and I want one of
you to begin, please, by taking this ordinary pack of cards
and removing the four Kings and the four Aces from the
pack. In fact, if you like, you can mark them with a pencil.

Now I'll put the four Aces on the table here, and the
four Kings on the table here, and at the same time you can
be examining the two envelopes. They are quite ordinary
too. Write 'Aces' on one and 'Kings' on the other. Thank
you.

Now I'll put the four marked Aces in the Aces envelope
and the four marked Kings in the Kings envelope; here is
one envelope for you to hold and the other for *you* to hold.

And now, believe it or not, I'm going to make the marked
Aces and Kings change places!

Let me open the envelopes and show you: the Aces are
now in the Kings envelope – and vice versa.

The Secret

You've been examining the pack of cards and the envelopes.
What you should have been examining is the table, or rather
the tablecloth. It's a dark colour – so dark you haven't
noticed those two oblongs on it!

They happen to be an Ace and a King whose backs are
the same colour as the tablecloth so they're invisible!
They're duplicates! (The easiest colour to use is probably
black; if you haven't got a black tablecloth, paint a large
sheet of paper black and lay it over the table. Use the same

paint to paint the backs of your two duplicate cards.)

When I collected the four Aces from you I put them on top of the *duplicate King*, and when I collected the four Kings I put them on top of the *duplicate Ace*!

I then asked you for your Kings envelope, picked up one group of cards, showed you the *duplicate King* and put it and the four Aces in the Kings envelope. Then I picked up the other group of cards, showing you the *duplicate Ace*, and put them in the Aces envelope.

When I take out the four Aces from the Kings envelope, and the four Kings from the Aces envelope, you won't ask to see the duplicate cards because you don't know they exist!

Four Star Magic ✳✳✳✳

These tricks are all ones used by professional magicians today. Performed properly, they will baffle any audience and earn you plenty of applause. In many ways the props needed for these tricks are even simpler than those needed for the Three Star Magic: to make a success of these particular tricks you need first really to understand them (read the explanations over and over again) and then really to perfect them (rehearse them over and over again).

When you read how a trick is done, the explanation may seem very complicated at first and there may seem to be an awful lot to remember. But if you take the tricks one stage at a time, and don't try to rush them, you'll be surprised how quickly you can master them.

Red, White and Blue

Props: Five special cards and a hat
Assistants: None
Helpers: None

The Trick

Here are three cards: one red, one white and one blue. I'll
put the three cards separately into this hat: red, white and
blue. And now I will take the red one and the white one
out of the hat and put them in my pocket. So what colour
is the card still in the hat?

Blue, you say? Well I know it's crazy, but it's *white* – see!
I'll slide it from my hat on to the table; there it is, the
white card.

So where has the blue one gone? It's here in my pocket.
I'll put it on the table; there it is, the blue card, along with
the red one from my pocket. Okay, so the white card must
be a trick card. Well, turn it over, because I can tell you
think it will be blue on the other side. But it isn't, is it? It's
white on both sides!

It's all very mysterious.

The Secret

Well, I *have* used a double-sided card, with one side white
and one blue, but I used it *early* on in the trick and then
dispensed with it. Let me run through the trick again:

I show you a red card, a white card and a card which
seems to be blue on both sides but is in fact white on the
back. I show the red both sides then drop it in the hat. I
show the white both sides then drop it in the hat. I have now
lulled your suspicions and I will in fact only show *one* side
of the blue card as I throw it casually into the hat.

Now I bring out the red, showing both sides. But when

I remove the 'white card' from the hat, I actually take out the trick card with only its white side showing. I now place these two cards into my pocket where the 'white card' is promptly exchanged for a real blue card – *blue on both sides* – which is in my pocket already!

So the white card found in the hat naturally turns out to be white on both sides and I'm able to produce a proper red card and a proper blue card from my pocket.

It always seems so simple once you know how it's done!

Find the Ace!

Props: Special playing cards and a stand for them
              about 30 cms long by 20 cms high
Assistants: None
Helpers: One

The Trick

I will quickly rest three cards (Ace, Jack and King) on this small stand made from a piece of wood covered in black velvet. So there are the three cards resting against the stand with their backs to us.

You saw me put the three cards down, so which is the Ace? The centre one? Are you sure? I'll pick it up and show you. No, the one you chose is the King.

Let's try again. I'll take the three cards off the stand and you shuffle them and, if you wish, examine them. Right, I will now quickly put the three cards on the stand again.

Which one is the Ace? You're sure it's the left-hand card? Alright, I'll turn it over. No, it's the Jack. You may *say* you were sure it was the Ace, but it isn't, is it? It's strange, but you don't seem to be able to find the Ace!

The Secret

On the black velvet stand I had already placed three cards, a King, Jack and *another* Jack. The secret of these three cards is that I had covered their backs with black velvet; although you are only a short distance away, your eyes cannot see this black velvet against the black velvet of the stand, as all the velvets have merged.

I then rested the three new cards on the stand *on top* of the three cards which were already resting there unnoticed by you. When I took off the centre card, which was the Ace, I also took off the card under it, which was not an Ace. The Ace was hidden by the card I showed you, the one with black velvet on its back.

As none of the three 'velvet-backed cards' is an Ace, you will *never* find the Ace while I'm in charge!

The Waistcoat and the Rope

Props: A waistcoat and a length of string about
            a metre long
Assistants: None
Helpers: None

The Trick

As you can see, I'm wearing a waistcoat and I've got this continuous loop of string, about a metre long, over my right arm. The loop is 'closed'. The fingers of my right hand are tucked into my waistcoat pocket.

There is no way I can get this loop of string free without taking my right hand from my waistcoat pocket, is there?

The Secret

You think I can't get the loop free without taking my right hand out of the waistcoat pocket – but you're wrong! To the Great Houdini all things are possible!

My right hand must stay in my waistcoat pocket, but with my left hand I pull the loop through the arm-hole of my waistcoat. I then pull it over my head. I then pull it out through the other arm-hole and over the other arm. I can now reach up under the waistcoat and pull the string down. It falls to the floor and I step out of it. I am free!

Your Three Cards

Props: A pack of cards
Assistants: One
Helpers: One

The Trick

You already know that the Great Houdini is a master of the art of mind reading, but did you know that he is also skilled in the art of 'thought transference'? I am now going to demonstrate to you how I can 'transfer' thoughts from my mind to the mind of my assistant.

I would like my assistant to go and stand at the far end of the room and I would like a volunteer from the audience to come up here and choose *three consecutive cards* from this pack and place the three cards in a row on the table. Fine.

It's quite impossible for me to know the cards, but I'll now look at them, think of them and transfer my thoughts to my assistant at the other end of the room. To make sure there is no trickery, my assistant has turned his back on us, as you see, so only thought transference can help him.

He will now name the three cards you chose!

The Secret

Let's look closely at the pack of cards: before the trick they've been secretly arranged in a certain special order; when you take away your chosen three cards, I will quite casually hold the top half of the pack (from the bottom of which the cards have been selected) with its face towards you – so my assistant can see the *bottom* card (of this top half) before he turns away.

He knows at once which three cards have been chosen by you because he knows which cards must follow that bottom one. And he knows that because he has learnt a 'code sentence'. Here it is:

*Eight kings threatened to save nine fair ladies for
one sick knave.*

That's an easy sentence to remember, and the interpretation
of the code is easy too: Eight (Eight) kings (King) threatened (Three Ten) to (Two) save (Seven) nine (Nine) fair
(Five) ladies (Queen) for (Four) one (Ace) sick (Six) knave
(Jack).

Because my assistant has learnt the sentence and the code
by heart, he only has to see one card to know all the cards
that follow it. As well as having each suit arranged in the
special order (Eight, King, Three, Ten, Two, Seven, Nine,
Five, Queen, Four, Ace, Six, Jack), my assistant knows that
the suits have been arranged in the order Diamonds, Spades,
Hearts, Clubs and can therefore tell you exactly what your
cards are.

A lot of tricks can be done by means of this code, so it's one
to learn well and never to forget!

The Magic Spell!

Props: A pack of cards
Assistants: None
Helpers: None

The Trick

This is a remarkable trick, and a useful one, too, because
it can be performed anywhere at any time; and the only
props needed are thirteen playing cards. To perform the
trick I take the thirteen cards and arrange them in such an
order as to enable me to *spell out* the cards in sequence from
the Ace right through to the King. I simply hold the
thirteen cards in my hand face downwards and I remove
one card from the top for each letter I spell out.

A–C–E spells 'Ace'; as I say *A* I remove the top card and place it face downwards at the bottom of the pack; as I say *C* I remove the second card and place it at the bottom of the pack; as I say *E* I remove the third card, and place *it* at the bottom of the pack. Having spelt A–C–E with the first three cards, I now say the whole word *Ace* and *turn over* the fourth card. Lo and behold, it is the Ace! I place the Ace to one side now because I have no further use for it and move on to Two.

I next spell out T–W–O and the fourth card – the one I turn over – will indeed be found to be a Two, so I put that on to one side on the table. And so on, right through to the time I spell out J–A–C–K, Q–U–E–E–N and K–I–N–G.

The Secret

Before starting the trick, I must arrange the cards in the following sequence: 3–8–7–Ace–Queen–6–4–2–Jack–King–10–9–5.

You will see that this arrangement *face down* makes Three the top card and Five the bottom card.

As I spell out the letters I make sure I move the top card to the bottom of the pile without disturbing the sequence of cards. The only cards I turn over are the ones I name; once I have named them I remove them from the pack. I remember not to disturb the sequence of cards and not to replace a removed card, but to put it down on the table and not use it again. If you do it properly, the trick never fails.

Houdini's Card Trick

Props: A playing card, an envelope, scissors, a
            needle and a length of ribbon
Assistants: None
Helpers: Two

The Trick

I call this Houdini's Card Trick because in the trick an
ordinary playing card – this Ace of Spades – is going to make
a miraculous escape from inside the envelope where it will
be held prisoner!

I need two volunteers from the audience to help guard
the card and see that it doesn't escape.

As you can see, here is the card, the Ace of Spades, and
I have cut a small hole just above its centre. Please examine
the card. Okay, so now I put the card in this envelope and
seal the envelope.

Now I take up this needle and push it through the
envelope, through the hole in the card and out of the other
side of the envelope. I have thus threaded this bit of ribbon
through the envelope and the card. I now want you to hold
each end of the ribbon and let the envelope hang on the
ribbon.

Now for the Houdini Escape! I take these scissors and cut
off one end of the envelope – and take the card out of the
envelope. The envelope is still threaded on the ribbon, yet
the card is free! Please, examine the envelope and the card,
there's no trick to it, is there?

The Secret

Of course there is! The envelope needs to be prepared
before the trick by cutting a slit at the bottom.

I then put the card in the envelope and seal the *top* end
of the envelope. But, I also squeeze the sides of the envelope

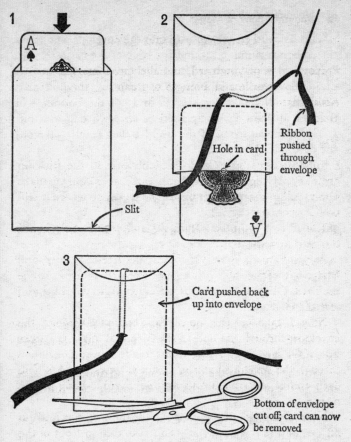

1 A♠

↓ (arrow)

Slit

2 Ribbon pushed through envelope

Hole in card

♠A

3 Card pushed back up into envelope

Bottom of envelope cut off; card can now be removed

as I hold it. The card will slide down and a little way out of the envelope, but my hand is hiding this and my little finger stops the card from falling on to the floor.

I push the needle through the centre of the envelope, though not through the card, of course, as the card is now below the centre of the envelope. I am holding the envelope in my left hand, so when I bring my right hand towards my left, I push the card up into the envelope with my right thumb.

This has pushed the card up into the envelope again and the ribbon is running around the edge of the card.

Now, to show both sides of the envelope, I'll turn it upside-down on the ribbon; as you can see, the bottom is now the top. I take the scissors and cut the bottom – in truth, I am cutting where there is *already* a cut and thus I've hidden the secret of the trick! I then simply take out the card and show it.

The Floating Glass

Props: A bottle of milk, a glass and thin wire or
             thread
Assistants: None
Helpers: None

The Trick

If I use ordinary household things for my magic, such as this bottle of milk and the glass on that table, then there can't be any trickery, can there?

Watch, I pick up the glass in one hand and the bottle of milk in the other. I hold the glass almost thirty centimetres below the bottle as I pour the milk out.

You're not going to believe this: I will now let go of the glass and it will float in the air, as, quite calmly, I continue to pour milk into it!

The Secret

Well, there is no trickery, but there is a piece of colourless thread. When you saw the bottle and the glass standing on the table, they were already joined by the thread.

I tie it round the lip of the bottle and – a bit harder, this – round the glass. To make sure the glass stays upright, I also tie a half-loop over the top of the glass, its two ends being knotted to the thread now tied round the glass.

When I lift up the bottle, the glass should hang about thirty centimetres below it. The glass must have sloping sides or the thread tied to it will slip up the glass.

All tricks involving thread will be spoiled if you let your audience get too close to you. Keep them at a distance, where they won't be able to see the thread, and they'll hardly believe their eyes.

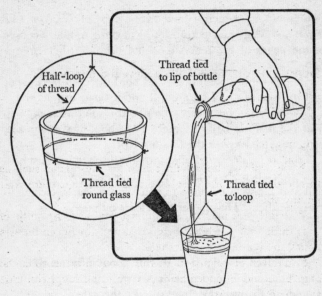

Half-loop of thread

Thread tied to lip of bottle

Thread tied round glass

Thread tied to loop

The Floating Ball

Props: A newspaper, a wooden hoop (about 30 cms
            in diameter) and a length of colourless
            thread
Assistants: None
Helpers: None

The Trick

Ladies and gentlemen, I have here a copy of *The New York Times* and, with your permission, I'm going to take a couple of the pages of the newspaper and crumple them into a ball.

And now – believe it or not – I hold the crumpled paper ball in front of me, I let go of it and it floats in mid air!

Not only that, but I can even pass this solid wooden hoop over the floating ball of paper! The hoop, as you can see, genuinely passes over the floating ball!

I can see you're watching hard and think there must be a trick somewhere, but there isn't. Let me hand over the paper ball and the wooden hoop to you. You're very welcome to examine them. That paper ball floats by magic.

The Secret

I got a piece of colourless thread about fifty centimetres long. One end I looped with a very small loop, just big enough to fit over my fingertip. At the other end of the thread was another loop, only larger. That one had to fit over my ear!

Before I began this illusion, I'd already slipped the thread over my ear – you didn't notice it because it then went round the back of my neck and was therefore hidden. I was then ready to start the trick.

I picked up the piece of newspaper; when I loosely crumpled it up in mid air, in actual fact I crumpled it up *around* the thread that now stretched from a fingertip on my right hand, round behind my neck, and was already looped on to my left ear.

As I moved my right hand, so the paper was made to rise and fall, seemingly in mid air. 'Just a minute,' you will say. 'You used that wooden hoop in the illusion. It obviously must be threaded on to the silk thread, otherwise you couldn't possibly pass the wooden hoop to and fro across the ball of paper. But how, without my noticing, did you thread the hoop on to the silk thread?'

I'll tell you. At the start, I had picked up the wooden hoop. Now, because I wanted to crumple up the paper with *both* hands, I had to put the hoop somewhere. So I casually decided to put it *over my head* and around my neck; as I did so, I threaded the invisible thread through the wooden hoop. This is really the basis of the illusion; this is what convinces you that there can be no thread anywhere,

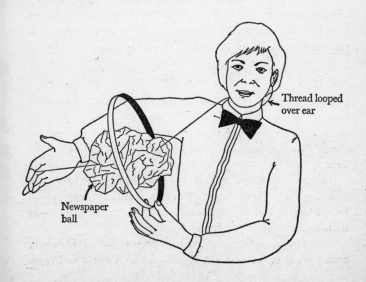

Thread looped over ear

Newspaper ball

for I just took the wooden hoop from off my head and could, of course, easily pass it to and fro over the 'floating ball'!

You don't need *The New York Times* for this trick – any paper will do – and you don't need a real wooden hoop, but you *do* need thread, fingers and fairly *big* ears!

Five Star Magic *****

Don't attempt any of the tricks in this chapter
until you have mastered all the other tricks and
illusions I have described so far. The tricks you will
find here are all ones you can do, but some of them
require rather special props and all of them require
skill on the part of the performer. When you have
constructed the props and mastered the art of
performing all these tricks you will have earned the
right to call yourself a Master of Magic.
Congratulations!

The Top Hat

Props: A special top hat and four silk handkerchiefs
Assistants: None
Helpers: None

The Trick

I expect you've been admiring my stylish top hat. It's smart, isn't it? And useful too. No magician should be without one.

As you can see, it's a perfectly straightforward hat on the outside with perfectly straightforward black lining on the inside. What's more, it's completely and utterly empty.

But if I make a magic pass over it, wave my magic wand and utter a few magic spells – look! It's no longer empty: it has one, two, three, four silk handkerchiefs coming out of it! I could even have taken a rabbit out in the famous traditional way! But how?

The Secret

If you look closely inside, the black lining material is covering the hat's interior *and* a hinged cardboard flap. I move the flap to one side; I can easily hide my handkerchiefs or rabbit behind it, can't I? Because the cardboard flap and the rest of the hat's interior are all of the same material, the flap is invisible when you are a few paces from it!

A trick top hat like this one is a very useful piece of equipment for any magician. And turning an ordinary second-hand top hat into a very special magician's one isn't difficult. You should be able to find an old top hat without too much trouble – in the attic, in a junk shop, at a jumble sale or on a second-hand clothes stall – and making the hidden false bottom only requires scissors, cardboard, black lining material and glue.

Magic Writing

Props: A small blackboard or slate, some sheets of
              newspaper, a cake of soap and some chalk
Assistants: None
Helpers: One

The Trick

For this mind-boggling piece of magic I am going to use
an old-fashioned slate, the sort that children used to do
their writing on at school. The trick works just as well with
a small, modern blackboard, but I prefer to do it the
traditional way – with a slate. Here is my slate; you are
most welcome to examine it on both sides. And here is a bit
of old newspaper. I now have to wrap the slate up in the
newspaper. It isn't easy, because the paper's so crumpled.
I'll smooth it out and then I can fold over the sides more
neatly. Right, I carefully fold the newspaper under the
slate and it's ready.

I put my fingertips lightly on the newspaper and think of
a message to write down – any message will do. What about
your name, sir? Let me concentrate on it for a moment. Now
I remove the newspaper and there, on the slate, your name
has been written – by magic!

The Secret

It isn't just 'a bit of old newspaper'. It is a bit of old
newspaper on which I have previously written your name
(in reverse, using mirror-writing) with the edge of a hard
piece of soap.

Then I covered the soap letters of your name with chalk
dust and crumpled up the newspaper (so the letters cannot
be seen) in preparation for meeting my audience.

When I mention to you that the sheet is crumpled and

needs straightening out, I smooth it out *firmly* – and thus press the chalk powder and soap letters onto the blank slate's surface.

I then remove the newspaper and reveal your name in 'magic' writing!

Waving the Flag

Props: A special paper tube, a special cardboard
           tube, six handkerchiefs and a flag
Assistants: None
Helpers: None

The Trick

I'll take this large sheet of paper, show you both sides of it, roll it up into a sort of tube and push three white handkerchiefs through it.

Amazingly – for you saw it was just a sheet of paper – the white handkerchiefs come out of the other end red, white and blue.

To achieve a really grand effect, I will now push these three coloured handkerchiefs through this different, larger and stronger tube of cardboard; look, they are transformed into the British flag! One minute a handkerchief, next minute the Union Jack!

The Secret

You will remember that I held up the sheet of paper (which shouldn't be too thin) and showed you both sides.

The front side I showed slowly, the back quickly, because I am holding the paper with my right hand loose, not tightly fisted. I don't want you to notice that my hand hides a fairly small tube of paper stuck on to the edge of the large sheet. I then rolled up the sheet of paper, held it as a

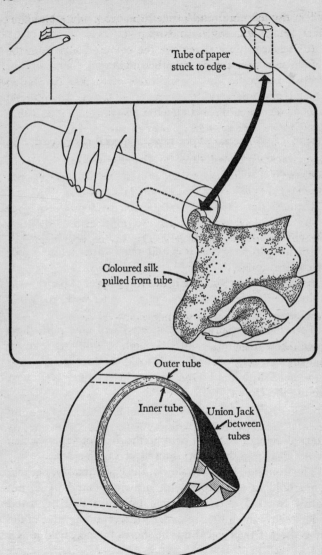

Tube of paper
stuck to edge

Coloured silk
pulled from tube

Outer tube

Inner tube

Union Jack
between
tubes

roll in my left hand and pushed the three white handkerchiefs into it with my right hand.

All I had to do was remove the coloured silks from the
hidden tube of paper at the other end!

With regard to the bigger tube of thicker cardboard
which is going to work the second effect for me, I don't hold
it too close to you but I do let you peer through it and thus
prove to you it is a 'hollow' tube of cardboard.

No wonder this second tube is made of thicker cardboard
– the thickness is really due to its being *two* tubes, one inside the other; carefully pushed into the small space between
the two tubes is a complete Union Jack.

If you perform this very spectacular trick properly, your
audience will be waving their programmes and shouting
'Bravo! *Encore*!' by the time you're waving your flag.

The Chinese Shawl

Props: A special shawl, paper flowers or
             handkerchiefs
Assistants: None
Helpers: None

The Trick

This lovely Chinese shawl I'm holding has a beautiful
oriental design on both sides, as you can see. In the middle
of the shawl is a tassel and as I hold it by the tassel the rest
of the shawl falls in drapes. I put my hand under the
drapes and somehow manage to produce one, two, three,
FOUR huge bouquets of flowers from nowhere!

The Secret

I mentioned that the shawl design is involved, and this
is deliberate. The design hides four tubes of similar material

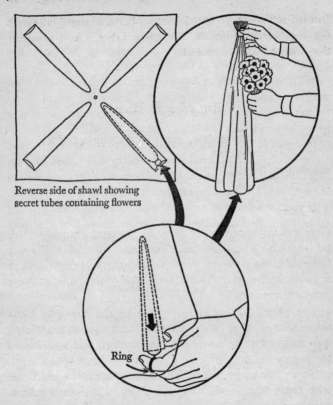

Reverse side of shawl showing
secret tubes containing flowers

Ring

to the shawl, sewn on to the shawl on the reverse side of the
tassel.

Now I put my hand inside the draped shawl and through
a ring. This ring is at the end of the artificial flowers that are
squeezed into the tubes. As I pull, the flowers come free and
at once become about five times the size they were when
compressed into the tubes. When all four bunches of
flowers are released, the effect is quite spectacular.

If you're no good at making paper flowers, don't worry.

Instead of flowers, you can hide tightly rolled multi-coloured silk handkerchiefs inside the secret tubes – and produce *them* with a flourish instead.

The Magic Box

Props: A special box, four handkerchiefs and a
             toy rabbit
Assistants: None
Helpers: None

The Trick

Here is a fancy cardboard box. As you see, I've closed the lid and sealed it with sticky paper. I have carefully cut three sides of a panel on the top of the box and three sides of a panel in the front of the box. The fourth side of these panels automatically becomes a hinge.

The panels are almost the size of the top and front respectively. Let us concentrate on the front panel, which I now pull out and downwards, the bottom side working as the hinge.

Now you can see inside. The interior is empty and lined with some attractively designed paper. I'll close the front panel.

Now I'll open the top panel and take from the box four large handkerchiefs and a toy rabbit! But the box was empty – you were sure it was!

The Secret

Placed in the box at an angle of forty-five degrees is a piece of mirror that fits the inside exactly. When I opened the front panel, you didn't really see the whole interior – you just saw half of it.

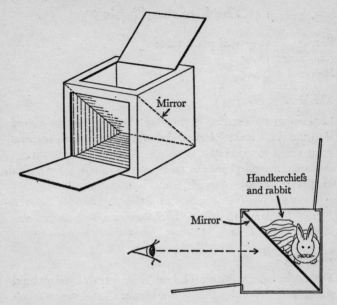

The other half was an illusion; what you saw was the floor reflected in the mirror; as the floor and the sides were all papered in the attractively designed paper, you thought the reflection of the floor in the mirror was the back wall.

Tucked in behind the mirror were the handkerchiefs and the toy rabbit! (Remember not to use *live* animals in your tricks; it is cruel.) Seeing is *not* believing – at least, not when a mirror is involved!

The Floating Table

Props: A special small table
Assistants: None
Helpers: None

The Trick

Ladies and gentlemen, if you don't yet believe the Great Houdini is a miracle-worker, you will in a moment, because I am about to make this table rise in the air and float!

I will now stand by the table, put my fingers lightly on its surface and concentrate; look! – the table rises!

What's more, it floats around as I command it!

Now I order it to sink to the floor again and, as you see, it does.

The Secret

The table *did* rise, didn't it? And, as you saw, I didn't hold the table; I merely rested my fingers on it – and they weren't glued to it either! So how did I make the table float at will?

I am wearing a ring on each hand; attached to each ring on the inside of my hand is a flat hook. Set into the table top are two small unseen clasp-like rings; as I lightly place my fingers on the table, I slide the unseen flat hooks forward into the unseen rings. As I lift my hands, so I lift the table!

For this trick, you can use an old coffee-table or even a very simple table you have made yourself. You may need help fixing the rings and hooks.

Above all, remember to keep your audience at a safe distance so that they don't see more than is good for them!

The Magic Table

Props: A special table and a golf ball
Assistants: None
Helpers: None

The Trick

Here's a genuine table of the type we conjurors always use.
As you can see, it's on a thin tripod base – there's no
trickery *there*; it also has a thin table-top covered in a bright
check pattern – to give a bit of colour to the act; there's
obviously no trickery there either. Finally, I'll flick the
fringe on the edge of the table for you – there, it's hiding
nothing.

I'll take my wand out of one pocket and a golf ball out of
the other and put them on the table. Now I'll hold them
both up for you to examine. Hey, where's the golf ball
gone? It's vanished! And look, I haven't palmed it, nor is
it up my sleeve! So where is it?

The Secret

The golf ball – or any other item you may want to make
vanish – was put down on the check tablecloth for a second.
It then disappeared. If you look closely at the check design
you will see that it isn't there to give a bit of colour to the
act at all – it's there because it has divided the table up into
squares of about five centimetres by five centimetres. One of
those squares – just a bit off centre – is in reality a hole;
under the hole is a bag, like you see at the corner of a billiard
table. And, of course, that's where the golf ball vanished to!

This table can be used to make all sorts of small objects
vanish – from golf balls to precious diamond rings. (If you
use valuable objects from members of the audience, remember to warn them that their possessions will be returned at
the end of the show. It's impossible to remove them from

the hole without the audience seeing – so get your assistant to slip them to you discreetly.)

A professional magician will have a table like this professionally made, but you can put together your own version of the 'Magic Table' without going to too much trouble or expense. You can even make one out of a very large cardboard box. Use the bottom of the box as the top of the table and paint a checked pattern of small squares on to the surface. Cut out just one of the squares and you can use the hole to make a wide variety of tiny objects disappear. (Black and white squares on the table-top work best in this trick.)

The Rabbit Cage

Props: A special cage and a toy rabbit
Assistants: None
Helpers: None

The Trick

Here is an empty rabbit cage with bars down the front. To prove to you that it really is empty, watch me lift off the roof and put my hand inside the cage.

But what use is a rabbit cage without a rabbit? I hold up my handkerchief in front of the cage, I take it away again – and there is the bunny in the cage!

The Secret

This is so simple! Let us look at the floor and walls inside the cage. They are all covered in black velvet – a muzzy material that confuses your eyes, because close inspection would show you that the cage is far smaller inside than it is outside!

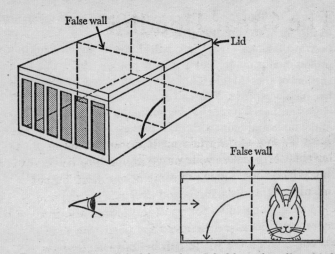

See, the back wall is false; when I held my handkerchief up close to the cage, I also held it up close to a catch. When I released the catch, the back wall flapped down and became a second floor – and the rabbit was revealed!

You obviously don't need to have a real rabbit cage. In fact, you could easily make your cage out of a cardboard box and paint it all black if you can't get hold of any velvet.

The Great Houdini

Don't try any of the tricks or illusions that are in this chapter – unless your name happens to be Harry Houdini! These are some of my most famous and difficult and daring – and *dangerous* – feats and I am describing them for you (and letting you into my secrets) because I believe that at last the time has come when the world can be told exactly how the Great Houdini did it!

The Sword Cabinet

Props: A special cabinet and a set of swords
Assistants: One
Helpers: None

The Trick

Ladies and gentlemen, this is one of the greatest magical illusions of all time. Let me open the door of this cabinet that stands on four legs and reveal a girl sitting inside. I now close the doors. I push three swords through one side of the cabinet and a further sword down through the top of the cabinet. This is cruel, for the girl must surely be pierced by the swords. In fact, what *has* happened to her?

I open the doors. There are all the swords thrust across the inside of the cabinet. As for the girl, she has vanished! Now I quickly close the doors, remove all the swords, open the doors again – and there she is once more! She has reappeared!

The Secret

Well, what did happen to the girl? She couldn't escape because the cabinet stood on four legs and was nowhere near any escape route: it wasn't standing close to any curtains or scenery or a trap-door in the floor.

The answer is that the girl has remained in the cabinet. The moment I close the doors, she slides two mirrors across in front of her. They meet at right angles; so that you will not see that angle, I push the sword through the cabinet roof directly in front of it.

The mirrors now reflect the side walls of the cabinet, which you think are the *back* wall.

It is easy for me to slide the various swords into the cabinet, in front of the two mirrors, so that when I open the

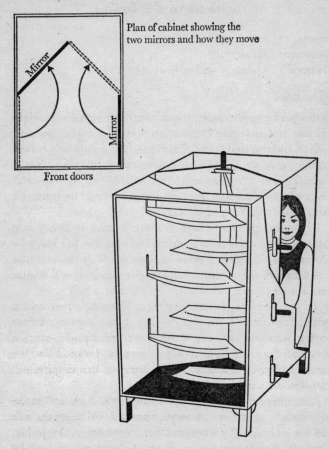

Plan of cabinet showing the
two mirrors and how they move

Mirror

Mirror

Front doors

doors you will see all the swords and – you think – the back
wall of the cabinet. The moment I have removed the
swords, the girl pushes aside the two mirrors that hide her
– and there she is, again in view!

Locked in the Safe

Props: A large safe
Assistants: An umpire
Helpers: A doctor and several others

The Trick

Ladies and gentlemen, as you know I am famous through-
out the world as the greatest escapologist there has ever
been. I believe that there is nothing that I couldn't escape
from – and that includes this massive safe, which the
manufacturers claim is the strongest, safest safe in the world.
They tell me that I shall never be able to escape from this
safe. I tell them they're wrong.

I have examined the safe thoroughly and so heavy is it
that special supports have been built under the stage to
prevent it collapsing! I must explain that this undertaking
is of a dangerous character and might fail. You will realize
that a man cannot breathe for long inside a safe.

As you can see, I am wearing a dressing-gown and a
bathing costume. I will remove my dressing-gown; before
getting into the safe I will be examined by a doctor; a
member of the public shall act as umpire. I would like the
doctor to search me thoroughly; perhaps the umpire will
examine the inside of the safe.

And, now that is done, may I thank you both and shake
your hands; as you return to your seats, I will enter the safe
and be locked in by various other members of the public
who will kindly remain on stage. A large screen will be
placed in front of the safe; if you hear a series of knocks, you
will know that it is a distress signal and that I wish to be
released, for I am not sure if I can conquer this particular
problem. However, with luck, the Great Houdini will
manage to escape from the safe in less than four minutes!

The Secret

I know perfectly well I can conquer this particular problem because the safe-makers themselves had asked me to examine the safe carefully and I had done so the night before. I had also carefully examined the new springs, which were so strong that I at once decided to replace them with springs of my own!

There had been one complication for me. I had agreed to wear just a swim-suit and so there was nowhere to hide the special key needed for the new and altered locking arrangements that had to be operated by me from the *inside*.

You will remember that I shook hands with the kind doctor and the umpire. The doctor was a doctor, but the umpire was one of my staff and I collected the special key as I shook hands with him. I then climbed in quickly before anyone noticed that I had the key.

When it comes to escaping from locked safes, I don't need magic; I just need locks I can pick and special keys to help me pick them.

Sawing the Lady in Half

Props: A wooden box and a saw
Assistants: Four
Helpers: None

The Trick

Ladies and gentlemen, I couldn't possibly leave you without presenting one of the most exciting and mysterious of all the great magical illusions. Before your very eyes, the Great Houdini is about to saw this young lady in half.

As you can see, my two assistants are each holding several wooden panels and will now piece the panels together on that table and construct an empty wooden box out of them. There it is, an empty wooden box with the lid open.

The young lady now steps into the box; you will see that at one end of the box there is a hole for her head. She puts her head through the hole, so. At the other end of the box she puts her feet through another hole. She is waving to you with her head and her feet as my assistants close the lid of the box.

Another of my assistants brings me a large saw. He and I find the rough centre of the box and we are soon sawing the box in half – and, yes, we are sawing the girl in half too!

You noticed that the box was empty. In fact, you saw this very simple box actually being constructed, but, even so, in case you think there could be some skulduggery, two of my assistants will now actually pull the two halves of the box apart.

There we are – all the fresh air you could wish for between the two halves of the box. The girl in the box is cut in half and, look! she waves her head at her feet and they wave back, although they have parted company!

My assistants now push the two halves close together again and the girl steps out of the box quite intact. She seems none the worse for her adventure.

The Secret

The secret is that there are really *two* secrets. The innocent-looking table seems to have the usual narrow top, but if you look closely at it you will see a thin line painted round it in a bright colour. Your eyes concentrated on that thin line and so did not notice the rest of the table's thickness which, in fact, is the thickness of a girl's body! Which brings me to the other secret. In the table itself is hidden a *second girl* who, once the box is constructed on the table, will lift her legs up through a panel in the bottom of the box and push her feet through the hole. When the two halves of the box are moved apart, her half will not be moved much but just slid about on the table top. All the while she will still be able to wiggle her feet.

The other half of the sawn box contains the entire body of the other girl, the one who you saw stepping into the box in the first place. She has drawn up her legs to squeeze into the smallest area possible, so *her* half can be moved about anywhere, taken any distance away from the other half of the box. You were mystified as to how her feet were able to

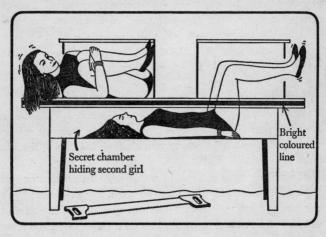

Secret chamber
hiding second girl

Bright
coloured
line

wave to the separated top half of her body, weren't you? Now you know – because they *weren't* her feet!

This is one of the great secrets of the world of magic – and never forget that the person who revealed it to you was none other than yours truly, the Great Houdini!

Walled in Alive!

Props: A stone wall
Assistants: Several
Helpers: Several masons

The Trick

Ladies and gentlemen, I am about to be walled in alive! Genuine masons are now building four walls of stone, which form an enclosed area, as you can see. It is like a room with no ceiling.

I now climb into this area and, in spite of the fact that stone is stronger than brick, I will soon escape and be amongst you again. You will appreciate that I cannot remove a stone from the wall, nor push one *out* from the wall, or the entire edifice will collapse on top of me.

If my assistants will place a screen against one of the walls – any wall will do – I will then make my escape.

The Secret

I cannot climb over the top, as the audience will see me. I cannot wriggle underneath, as the wall has been set into a concrete base. It is no exaggeration to say that I am 'walled in alive'.

The first secret of this escape is that my assistants, although pretending to let the audience decide in front of which wall the screen shall be placed, have in fact placed the screen around one particular wall – indeed around one particular

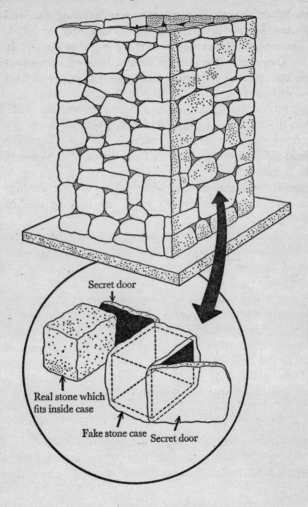

Secret door

Real stone which
fits inside case

Fake stone case   Secret door

stone. When the genuine masons were building the wall they were 'helped' by my assistants who, during the building, handed them yet another heavy stone to be put in place. This particular stone is in fact hollow, with secret doors at each end, though for the moment it is weighted down with another stone inside it to fool the masons.

Once the screen is in place and hiding me and the walls, I open the secret door to the fake stone, remove the heavy real stone, wriggle through the hollow stone, fasten the secret door from the outside and step forward to take my bow.

I am quite happy if the public ask to inspect the four walls because the false stone's panel can only be opened from the inside.

START HERE IF YOU WANT TO BE A BLACK BELT IN KARATE

START HERE IF YOU WANT TO BE A WORLD-CHAMPION RACING DRIVER

START HERE IF YOU WANT TO GO SKIN-DIVING

START HERE IF YOU WANT TO PADDLE YOUR OWN CANOE

Peter Little and David English

Ideal books to introduce these exciting sports – from the fascinating world of the deep to the inside view of motor racing.

THE PUFFIN BOOK OF TENNIS

Brian Glanville

Since its early days as a pastime for bored monks, tennis has become a fascinating game for players and spectators of all ages. In this book you can read about the top players who have thrilled, angered and inspired.

CARS, BOATS, TRAINS AND PLANES
CASTLES, CHURCHES AND HOUSES

Alan Jamieson

Two books designed to help children recognize objects and buildings they see when travelling about the country-side and towns, on holiday or in a car.

THE PUFFIN BOOK OF HANDWRITING

Tom Gourdie

How to write in a beautiful cursive style.

Heard about the Puffin Club?

... it's a way of finding out more about Puffin
books and authors, of winning prizes (in
competitions), sharing jokes, a secret code, and,
perhaps seeing your name in print! When you
join you get a copy of our magazine, *Puffin
Post*, sent to you four times a year, a badge
and a membership book.

For details of subscription and an application
form, send a stamped addressed envelope to:

The Puffin Club Dept A
Penguin Books Limited
Bath Road
Harmondsworth
Middlesex UB7 ODA

and if you live in Australia, please write to:

The Australian Puffin Club
Penguin Books Australia Limited
P.O. Box 257
Ringwood
Victoria 3134